East Lancashire Railway Recollections
David Mather

© David Mather 2015

All rights reserved. No part of this publication may be reproduced, stored in a retrieval system or transmitted, in any form or by any means, electronic, mechanical, photocopying, recording or otherwise, without prior permission in writing from Silver Link Publishing Ltd.

First published in 2015

British Library Cataloguing in Publication Data

A catalogue record for this book is available from the British Library.

ISBN 978 1 85794 456 3

Silver Link Publishing Ltd
The Trundle
Ringstead Road
Great Addington
Kettering
Northants NN14 4BW

Tel/Fax: 01536 330588
email: sales@nostalgiacollection.com
Website: www.nostalgiacollection.com

All photographs are the author's copyright unless otherwise credited.

Printed and bound in the Czech Republic

Frontispiece: **SUMMERSEAT** 'Black 5' No 45407 approaches Summerseat station on 5 April 2009. *Tom Jeffs*

Contents

Introduction	3
ELR beginnings	7
Heywood	9
Burrs Country Park and the Irwell Sculpture Trail	14
Bury and Bolton Street station	16
Bury to Ramsbottom	20
Ramsbottom to Rawtenstall	31
Special events	38
Stock	44
Bury Transport Museum	46
Future plans	48
Index	48

Acknowledgments

I would like to offer my sincere thanks to the many photographers who have generously allowed me to use their work in this book, and to those fellow enthusiasts who have given so freely of their time, knowledge and advice during its production. Special mention must go to Geoff Cryer and Phil Horton for granting permission to include their images. Gratitude is also due to the unsung heroes – the volunteers whose enthusiasm helps to make visiting the East Lancs Railway such a pleasure.

About the author

David Mather has been a lifelong railway enthusiast, from the steam days of the 1950s and '60s through to the present. Born and brought up in industrial Lancashire, his local 'patch' was centred on Bolton, with its busy shed, coded 26C (later 9K), its routes to Manchester and Blackburn and, of course, to the West Coast Main Line. Following his graduation from Birmingham University and a time spent teaching in the West Midlands, he moved back to the North of England, albeit to the other side of the Pennines. After taking early retirement from his successful career in science teaching in the historic railway city of York, he now devotes more time to his leisure interests, prominent among which had always been railways and photography. The digital revolution afforded the opportunity to bring his large stock of negatives and slides back to life and, in association with Silver Link Publishing, this led to a series of railway titles starting with *Running out of Steam: The photographic diary of a teenage railway enthusiast, 1966-68* (published in 2010 with a Foreword by Ian Allan). This was quickly followed by *Riding the Settle & Carlisle* (2011), *Great Britain's Heritage Railways* (2012) and *The Railways of York* (2014). Further works are in preparation.

Introduction

In a style of which the Victorian railway builders would have been proud, and after waiting for more than 18 years, the East Lancashire Railway Preservation Society celebrated the sweetest of days when the East Lancashire Railway was well and truly opened on 25 July 1987.

To satisfy the demands of mill owners in the Irwell Valley for a more efficient transport system to connect them with the increasingly important industrial hub of Manchester by replacing inadequate roads and frustratingly slow canals, the Act of Parliament authorising construction of the railway line was obtained in 1844 by the Manchester, Bury & Rossendale Railway Company, which was absorbed into the East Lancashire Railway Company (ELR) the following year. The railway began at Clifton near Salford, from where it ran north through a cutting at Outwood, then north-east through Radcliffe Bridge, Withins and on to Bury. Leaving Bury, the line continued through Summerseat, Ramsbottom and Stubbins to Rawtenstall, climbing constantly across embankments and viaducts and through cuttings and tunnels. The impressive Clifton Viaduct carried the line over the River Irwell and the Manchester, Bolton & Bury Canal. During its short life the ELR grew to include Liverpool, Manchester, Preston and Blackburn, as it absorbed several of its competitors including the Blackburn & Preston Railway and the Liverpool, Ormskirk & Preston Railway, which gave it direct access to Liverpool Docks.

The first line was completed and opened in 1846. The rather grand Bury station (later named Bury Bolton Street when Knowsley Street station on the Bolton to Rochdale line was opened) became the company's headquarters, and in 1848 a branch was created from Stubbins to Accrington, followed in 1852 by an extension of the main line from Rawtenstall to Bacup as the ELR increased its influence in the area, only to be amalgamated into the growing Lancashire & Yorkshire Railway empire in 1859.

CLIFTON The impressive Clifton Viaduct was built across the Manchester, Bolton & Bury Canal and the River Irwell, which flowed 80 feet (24 metres) below. Its largest span is 96 feet (29 metres). The trackbed between Clifton and Radcliffe now forms part of the Irwell Sculpture Trail, but unfortunately there is no public access across the viaduct, which is a Grade II Listed structure. *'Parrot of Doom'*

Visiting the East Lancashire Railway

Britain's heritage railways continue to attract and inspire, and the East Lancs Railway, with its lovingly restored stations and authentic atmosphere, is at the forefront of today's thriving preservation movement. Its variety of traction and rolling stock and the ever-friendly welcome of its staff make each visit a joy that has had led the author and many more like him to return for more.

Sat-nav postcodes for ELR stations:

Heywood	OL10 1LX
Bury	BL9 0EY
Summerseat	BL9 5QY
Ramsbottom	BL0 9AL
Irwell Vale	BL0 0QG
Rawtenstall	BB4 6AG

The ELR used a variety of locomotives in its early days, including 'long-boiler' 2-2-2s from Fenton, Craven & Co, at least one of which was used at the inauguration of the railway, though they were later rebuilt as 2-4-0s by R. & W. Hawthorn. Several 0-6-0 locos were also used on the railway, early examples being supplied in the 1840s mainly by the Haigh Foundry near Wigan. A successful and widely adopted wheel arrangement for both tender and tank locomotives, later examples were designed by Kirtley and Johnson for the Midland Railway (MR), Webb for the London & North Western (LNWR) – his 'Coal Engines' – and Barton Wright and Aspinall for the Lancashire & Yorkshire Railway (LYR).

The outside-frame 2-4-0 series were the largest class of locos operated by the ELR and, though some were later converted to 2-4-0 tank engines (and one to a 2-4-0 saddle tank), they were among the last locomotives to be built in Bury. The company's livery for its passenger locomotives was dark green with red-brown frames and polished domes and safety valves.

The 2-4-0 became the standard loco type for passenger and mixed traffic work and was used on most UK railways between 1846 and 1880. It included designs by Kirtley for the MR and Webb for the LNWR. Webb's later 2-4-0 design, the 'Improved Precedents' or 'Jumbos', were to number more than 150 locos, including the now preserved No 790 *Hardwicke*, which achieved record speeds during the 'Race to the North' in the 1890s.

With the decline of the

Above: Some of the early 0-6-0 designs stood the test of time by surviving into BR days; this former LYR Class '27' locomotive, designed by Aspinall and seen here at Ramsbottom, has been preserved and is running on the ELR as LMS No 12322 while on loan from the Ribble Steam Railway, Preston.

Below: Webb's 2-4-0 loco No 790 *Hardwicke* in 1907. In 1895 she set a new speed record when she covered the 141 miles (227km) between Crewe and Carlisle in 2hr 6min, with an average speed of 67.1mph (108km/h).

An early example of an outside-frame 2-4-0 of a type that might have graced the infant East Lancashire Railway is this loco, built to a design by Kirtley around 1870.

traditional cotton industry, and in the face of increasing competition from road transport, the rail service inevitably suffered and, following the recommendations contained in Dr Beeching's now infamous report published in 1963, 'The Reshaping of British Railways', eventually ceased. Of the former ELR routes, first to go in 1966 was the Accrington branch, quickly followed by the Rawtenstall to Bacup section. In 1972 the line lost its passenger service north of Bury, with freight in the form of coal to a depot at Rawtenstall stopping in 1980, the year that finally saw the closure of the Bury Bolton Street to Rawtenstall branch. The Bolton to Rochdale line had also closed, which left the electrified section south to Manchester as Bury's only surviving rail passenger service. In 1980 the Town Council, eager to improve links with road transport to and from the town, decided that the solution lay in building a new transport interchange comprising a bus and railway station roughly on the site of the old Knowsley Street station, thereby rejuvenating the town's road and rail infrastructure.

The closure of the Accrington branch prompted the formation of the East Lancashire Railway Preservation Society, though little progress was made in those early years other than to develop a museum-style depot at the old goods yard and shed adjacent to Bolton Street station. Thus the Bury Transport Museum was born, and a variety of road and rail vehicles was gradually amassed and developed into what is now a wide-ranging collection. However, the eventual operation of the reinstated ELR was always a major aim, and when BR's use of the line ceased it was just the fillip needed for the society's entry into the world of timetabled railway operation, aided by the considerable advantage of acquiring a line still in place and, until 1980, still in operation by BR. With massive practical and financial support from Councils throughout the area, from the Department of the Environment and others, the railway was reborn. Always ambitious, plans to extend the 4-mile run from Bury to Ramsbottom to Irwell Vale (6.5 miles), then on to Rawtenstall (8 miles) were no pipe-dream. After only 8 days of operation more than 10,000 passengers had been carried by the eight-trains-daily service, including, most encouragingly, a growing number of regular Saturday shoppers from Ramsbottom to Bury. The new railway was actually doing very nicely.

The mainstay of motive power in those early days was ex-CEGB 0-6-0T No 1 (RSH 7683/51), purchased from Meaford Power Station near Stone, Staffordshire, and former Manchester Ship Canal Railway 0-6-0T No 32 *Gothenburg* (HC 680/03). Other 'industrials' in the fleet included former North Western Gas Board 0-4-0ST No 1 (AB 1927/27) and ex-NCB 'Austerity' 0-6-0ST No 8 *Bickershaw* (Hunslet 3776/52), renamed *Sir Robert Peel* by the ELR. Main-line steam was represented by Stanier 'Black 5' 4-6-0 No 45337 and BR Standard Class 4 tank No 80097, though both were 'non-runners' undergoing restoration in 1987. BR Standard Class 5 No 73156, BR Class 9F No 92207 and Ivatt Class 2 No 46428 were also awaiting their turn for attention. The early diesel fleet was more impressive, including 'Warship' Class No D832 *Onslaught*, 'Western' Class No D1041 *Western Prince*, 'Hymek' No D7076, and Class 40 No 40145, as well as several industrial diesels. Coaching stock was made up of ex-BR Mark 1s, which were being repaired and restored to early-1960s-style maroon livery.

One of the pioneers of ELR workings, this Robert Stephenson & Hawthorn 0-6-0T, Works No 7683/51, hauled some of the first trains from Bury as No 1. She has been repainted in blue livery and carries the name *Ted Garrett JP, DL, MP. Stevie 742*

On that historic Saturday in July 1987, a large crowd of enthusiastic supporters witnessed the Mayor of Bury perform the opening ceremony and declare Bury Bolton Street station and the ELR reopened. A six-coach train double-headed by Hudswell Clark No 32 *Gothenburg* and RSH No 1 then carried the invited guests to Ramsbottom, where an even larger crowd saw the Mayor of Rossendale conduct further formalities before the VIP 'Special' returned to Bury. Regular weekend operating followed, with passenger numbers more than justifying the resolve and commitment shown by all the parties involved in bringing the East Lancashire Railway back to life.

Above left: BR 'Western' Class diesel-hydraulic No D1041 *Western Prince* stands at Bury during August 1998. *Phil Horton*

Left: Seen prior to preservation, NCB Hunslet 'Austerity' 0-6-0ST No 8, Works No 3776/52, was later renamed *Sir Robert Peel* when working on the reopened ELR. *Geoff Cryer*

Above: Ex-Manchester Ship Canal Railway 0-6-0T No 32 *Gothenburg* waits at Bury Bolton Street station with a 'Special' for Ramsbottom, the 'Irwell & Mersey Rambler', on 29 October 1987. *Geoff Cryer*

The extension to Rawtenstall was opened in April 1991 and, as passenger numbers continued to increase, requiring longer trains to be hauled up the testing gradients, more pulling power was clearly needed. The company responded by progressively increasing its stock of more powerful locomotives so that within a few short years the list of steam locos that could call this stretch of line their home included two more LMS 'Black 5s', Nos 44871 and 45407, LMS 'Crab' 2-6-0 No 42765, GWR 2-8-0 No 3855 and 2-8-2T No 7229, SR 'Battle of Britain' Class No 34073 *249 Squadron* and 'Merchant Navy' No 35009 *Shaw Savill*, LNER 'B12/2' 4-6-0 No 61572, and the unique BR 8P 'Pacific' No 71000 *Duke of Gloucester* – an impressive stock list by any standard, and one that does not include the diesels and 'industrials'.

In recent years a major project for the ELR has been the 'missing link' extension to Heywood, thereby connecting with the national network. After a long period of negotiation to overcome complex legal and statutory problems, the Bury to Heywood section was finally opened to passenger services on 3 September 2003, with a further short length of 500 metres beyond the newly built Heywood station over Green Lane level crossing to Hopwood, allowing locomotive and stock exchange with the national network to be achieved, and giving the ELR an impressive 12 miles of line to Rawtenstall.

Over time the return for the backers has been the development of this part of Lancashire, and of the Upper Irwell Valley in particular, as a major leisure area, reviving the economy of East Lancashire. With its attractive scenery, historic small towns and cultural heritage, the region is well placed to attract visitors from far and wide, with the resurgent railway as an essential and integral part of this development.

ELR beginnings

The East Lancashire Railway Preservation Society entered the field of railway preservation very late, more than 20 years after the withdrawal of BR passenger services over the line, and although the great determination of those early 'movers and shakers' was eventually rewarded, the stretch of line preserved was not that which had been originally intended.

Formed in 1966, the original group was named The Helmshore & District Railway Preservation Society, and its intention was to preserve the section of line between Stubbins Junction and Accrington. Progress, however, was painfully slow, the few activists being hampered by insufficient funds and a distinct lack of cooperation from the local Haslingdon Corporation. In spite of this, and encouraged by two successful Gala Days, the second of which in 1970 featured LMS 'Black 5' No 44806 in steam and attracted 3,500 visitors, the society persevered, though by 1971 it had become evident that there was to be no future for its base at Helmshore, especially as by then BR had started to lift the tracks. The search for an alternative site for the small but growing stock began in earnest, and eventually the former East Lancashire Railway warehouse at Castlecroft, Bury, was selected. A one-year lease was negotiated with Bury Council, and in May 1972 the stock was moved from Helmshore, and the Bury Transport Museum was created.

It was at this time that passenger services between Bury and Rawtenstall were withdrawn, but BR was unsympathetic to any plans to

The much-travelled 'Black 5' No 44806 was one of the ELR's early attractions. *Andy Dingley*

operate preserved rolling stock over the line. More stock continued to arrive at the museum during the ensuing years and, though coal trains continued to operate to Rawtenstall during this period, these were somewhat surprisingly halted by BR in December 1980. This provided the trigger for the society to initiate a meeting with BR's representatives, together with others from the Greater Manchester, Lancashire, Bury and Rossendale Councils, with the object of persuading the 'powers that be' that a light railway along the valley would be of great benefit to the area. Now the Councils were supportive, so much so that BR agreed to postpone lifting the tracks.

To 'test the water', a charter train was organised to run on 27 March 1982, the costs being met by Greater Manchester Council (GMC). In fact, three trains ran with great success, carrying 1,300 passengers including the council representatives, and the museum was visited by 2,000 people. Financial support quickly followed, with funding obtained by the GMC from the Derelict Land Grant to enable the purchase of the land from BR, and though much of the track was in a very poor state and four bridges needed to be replaced, a Light Railway Order was applied for in 1985. The project continued to be supported by the Metropolitan Borough of Bury after the GMC was abolished in March 1986, and the first works train ran to Summerseat on 27 December of that year. From then on the rate of progress was dramatic, with the opening train running to Ramsbottom on 25 July 1987. On 31 May 1988 the first works train reached Irwell Vale, and on 5 November a similar train arrived at Rawtenstall, the terminus of the 'extension'. Both trains were hauled by the ex-North West Gas Board Andrew Barclay 0-4-0ST No 1, built in 1927.

The Rawtenstall extension was reopened to passengers on 27 April

RAMSBOTTOM This is Ramsbottom station on 7 March 1977. In its original form the line through the station was double-track and there were two platforms, but from April 1970 the southbound line was lifted and the northbound platform became bidirectional. To facilitate this the goods shed, station buildings and footbridge were demolished and a simple 'bus shelter' erected on the former northbound platform. The station was closed in 1972, but the 'new' ELR rebuilt it, reconstructing the southbound platform together with the station buildings in their original style. As time progressed a canopy and footbridge were added, together with LMS-style gas lamp standards and BR (LMR)-style totems, recreating an authentic 1950s atmosphere at what is now a most attractive station.

STUBBINS The station at Stubbins, between Ramsbottom and Ewood Bridge on the East Lancashire Railway's line from Clifton Junction to Rawtenstall via Bury, was photographed on the same day. Officially opened in January 1847, the line through the station was originally double-track, with two platforms on an embankment, so that a two-storey booking office was required with the entrance at road level and steps up to the platforms. Later, in 1848, the ELR's Accrington line began from a junction just south of the station, to become the company's main line, with the line through the station to Rawtenstall becoming a secondary branch. The station was closed in June 1972 and the buildings demolished, though the platforms remained in situ. The Accrington line was also lifted at about this time. With the reopening of the Bury to Rawtenstall line by the 'new' ELR, consideration was given to reinstating the station, but these plans were later dropped, though the platforms still remain.

Heywood and Buckley Wells

Andrew Barclay 0-4-0ST No 1 is now housed in the Bury Transport Museum.

1991, the train being hauled by the same two locos that had been in charge of the 'Opening Special' to Ramsbottom four years earlier – a fitting reward to the dedicated few who had battled for 20 years against all odds. Attention then turned to the other end of the line, where the vital connection to the national network by way of Heywood had to be re-established in order to attract visiting locos and excursion traffic. This second extension would involve a new bridge and approach embankments to carry the track over the Metrolink line at Bury, as well as a replacement bridge at Broadfield to cross Pilsworth Road. Another long battle was about to begin…

Heywood is a small factory town with a big industrial past. Many of the mills in the vicinity are still evident to this day, reminders of the area's importance in the cotton trade during the Industrial Revolution. It is situated on the south bank of the River Roch and nearby is the Grade II-listed 'Queens Park', which was presented to the people of the town by Queen Victoria in 1879. Among its many attractions are a lake and riverbank walk, a cafe and visitor centre, wetland and wildlife areas, toilets and a free car park. With the impressive scenery of the Pennines close by and just a few miles from Manchester, Heywood is a convenient starting point from which to explore the ELR and its surrounding area.

The Heywood extension was yet another challenge for the stalwarts of the ELR, but one that had to be overcome in order to connect with the national network and allow visiting engines to add their 'pulling power' to the heritage line's programme of events. With the expertise of Bury Metropolitan Council's engineers, a new bridge was completed to carry the Heywood extension over the Metrolink line before trams started to run between Manchester and Bury on 6 April 1992. A second bridge over Pilsworth Road was also completed in time to permit visiting locos to take part in the ELR's celebrations to mark the 25th anniversary of the end of steam on BR in August 1993. The 20 acres of derelict railway land at Buckley Wells had been acquired from BR that year, complete with its Grade II-listed carriage shed. In view of the planned integration of the Metrolink and ELR services, it was a strategically important site, being close to the proposed Metrolink park and ride station. Buckley Wells played host to an array of visiting locos during that event, many of which would be used on trains during their stay on the railway. However, repairs to track and structures, resignalling at Bury Bolton Street and the construction of the new station at Heywood, not to mention the complex legal and statutory requirements involved, meant that it would be another ten years before passenger trains could operate over the extension to Heywood.

BUCKLEY WELLS Locos on display for the 1993 gala included GWR 2-8-0s Nos 3822 and 2857. *Phil Horton*

BUCKLEY WELLS Another attraction was LMS 2MT 2-6-0 No 46441. *Phil Horton*

BUCKLEY WELLS LMS 4F 0-6-0 No 4422 is seen on the same day. *Phil Horton*

BUCKLEY WELLS Here we see BR Standard 4MT 2-6-0 No 76079 with GWR 'Modified Hall' No 6998 *Burton Agnes Hall*. *Phil Horton*

BUCKLEY WELLS Somerset & Dorset Joint Railway 7F 2-8-0 No 53809 was also at Buckley Wells. *Phil Horton*

East Lancashire Railway Recollections

BUCKLEY WELLS Finally, this is BR 9F 2-10-0 No 92203. *Phil Horton*

Above: **HEYWOOD** This is the approach to Heywood station from Green Lane. Situated on the town's Railway Street, Heywood station is the beginning of the line. It is a manned station with a large free car park, toilets (including disabled) and a small waiting room.

At last, on 6 September 2003, the Bury to Heywood section of the railway was opened to regular passenger services, with a further short section beyond the station over Green Lane level crossing to the boundary, with the national network at Castleton being used for the exchange of locomotives and stock.

Above: **HEYWOOD** At Heywood the locos must run round their trains for the return journey, often topping up with water in the process.

HEYWOOD GWR 4-4-0 No 3717 (originally No 3440) *City of Truro* is seen at Heywood station on 27 July 2007. *Raymond Knapman*

After leaving Heywood, the line descends Broadfield Bank and crosses the M66 motorway and the River Roch before climbing towards Bury town centre and the Irwell Valley.

Visiting 9F 2-10-0 No 92214 heads a Bury to Heywood service in April 2008. *David Ingham*

Burrs Country Park and the Irwell Sculpture Trail

Burrs Country Park, a 36-hectare park alongside the River Irwell on the outskirts of Bury offers good facilities for walking, picnicking, birdwatching and fishing.

Once the site of a large cotton mill, it has been transformed from a derelict industrial wasteland into an attractive modern country park. It contains the feeder canal for Elton Reservoir, which in turn is the source of water for the Manchester, Bolton & Bury Canal. The canal fell into decline with the coming of the railway and was eventually abandoned in 1961, though its route has been protected from any adverse development that might prevent its restoration. The Manchester, Bolton & Bury Canal Society was formed in 1987 with the aim of restoring and reopening the waterway, the first stage of which was completed in 2008.

BURRS COUNTRY PARK Birds such as the grey heron have returned to the Irwell Valley, testament to the water quality in this once polluted river. *Kametan70*

BURRS COUNTRY PARK The feeder canal for Elton Reservoir flows through the park, carried on an aqueduct over the River Irwell. *Dennis Turner*

East Lancashire Railway Recollections

Burrs Country Park also contains part of the Irwell Sculpture Trail, the largest public art scheme in the UK. The 30-mile (48km) footpath follows the Irwell Valley from Salford Quays through Bury into Rossendale and on into the Pennines above Bacup. Since 1987 more than 30 pieces of public art have been commissioned from regional, national and international artists. The Country Park is also the venue for Bury Agricultural Show, held annually in June.

Above: **MOUNT SION** The Grade II-listed steam crane at Mount Sion on the Bury Arm of the Manchester, Bolton & Bury Canal was used to collect loads from the canal boats and transfer them to the nearby yard. *'Parrot of Doom'*

Left: **IRWELL SCULPTURE TRAIL** The collection of public artwork along the trail includes 'Tilted Vase' by Edward Allington, on display at Ramsbottom. *Nick Smale*

Right: **IRWELL SCULPTURE TRAIL** 'Trinity' is a tribute to the many navvies who laboured (and often perished) digging the Outwood Cutting near Radcliffe during the construction of the original railway line. *'Parrot of Doom'*

Bury and Bolton Street station

The bustling town of Bury was once an important centre for the Lancashire cotton industry, with the nearby Brooksbottom Mill in Summerseat playing a major role in launching the town's success. Its importance grew further with its connection to the national canal system in the early 19th century by means of the Manchester, Bolton & Bury Canal.

The town is renowned as the birthplace of Sir Robert Peel, founder of the British police force, who is commemorated by a monument at the Parish Church in the town centre and by the impressive 'Peel Tower', which dominates the skyline above Ramsbottom near the village of Holcombe.

Bury's famous market is a major attraction, with visitors coming from all over the UK, often by coach, to browse the vast array of stalls, many offering fresh produce and local delicacies including the well-known 'Bury black pudding'.

The town's Bolton Street station is the headquarters of the 'new' ELR. It dates back to 1846 when, as plain Bury station, it was also the headquarters of the original company of that name. When the ELR became part of the Lancashire & Yorkshire Railway in the 1880s the station was rebuilt, and the existing platform canopy dates from that time. After the Second World War the street frontage

BURY The statue of Sir Robert Peel (1788-1850) by Edward Hodges Baily stands in Bury Market Place. Born in the town, Peel rose to become Prime Minister and is best remembered for the repeal of the 'Corn Laws' and for the introduction of the modern police force (hence the terms 'Bobbies' and 'Peelers'). *David Ingham*

Left: **BURY BOLTON STREET** The station entrance on Bolton Street.

Above: **BURY BOLTON STREET** The layout of the station can be seen beyond the restored signal gantry. Platform 1, the bay platform, is to the right, and the line to Rawtenstall runs through Bolton Street Tunnel straight ahead. The station, like the railway as a whole, is run almost entirely by volunteers.

burned down and was replaced in 1952 by a brick and concrete entrance. There are four platforms: Platform 1 is a bay platform at the south-east end; Platform 2, the up platform on the east side, now boasts a new building incorporating a facade from the former Bury tram depot; Platform 3 is the down platform, being one side of an island platform; and Platform 4, the other side of the island platform next to the western retaining wall, is bidirectional. There are toilet facilities, the Trackside Bar and the Buffet for refreshments, with ample 'pay & display' parking next to the station.

The railway operates a service at weekends throughout the year, and every day except Mondays and Tuesdays between April and September. Please refer to the website at www.eastlancsrailway.org.uk for timetables and fares.

Left: **BURY BOLTON STREET**
Situated on Platform 2, the Trackside Bar serves a variety of tasty Lancashire fayre and drinks.

Below left: **BURY BOLTON STREET**
For the model railway enthusiast, a well-stocked shop at the northern end of Platform 2 holds a wealth of items for keen modellers to add to their layouts.

Below: **BURY BOLTON STREET**
Stanier 'Black 5' No 45407 simmers gently before taking its train away from Bolton Street station in August 1998. *Phil Horton*

BURY SOUTH SIGNAL BOX

The line to Heywood branches to the left behind the photographer, while the lines to the right ran to Manchester Victoria until closure by BR in 1991. Originally intended to provide a connection between ELR to BR metals, they now operate as sidings for the heritage railway. Beyond them is part of the Light Rapid Transit system (Manchester Metrolink), which opened on 6 April 1992, the connection with the national network having been formed by the more recent Heywood extension.

BURY SOUTH SIGNAL BOX The interior in October 2009. *ELR S&T Dept*

Bury to Ramsbottom

On leaving Bury, the line begins the long climb up the valley by way of Ramsbottom, crossing the River Irwell nine times before reaching the terminus at Rawtenstall. From Heywood to Rawtenstall, the journey of more than 12 miles takes approximately an hour in each direction, providing the opportunity to admire some of the beautiful scenery on the way.

After almost 3 miles of steady climbing at 1 in 132, we reach the unstaffed halt at Summerseat. This tiny station is located at Railway Road in the village, but motorists should be aware that the road to the station is very narrow with a few passing places. The station once boasted attractive buildings, a footbridge over the then double track, a signal box and goods sidings. Sadly these are long gone, and although there is a small car park for about six cars there are no refreshment or toilet facilities.

SUMMERSEAT station is seen here in the 1920s, before the footbridge was erected to replace the barrow crossing.

SUMMERSEAT Having just departed from Summerseat station, LNER 'K4' No 61994 *The Great Marquess* continues the steady climb towards Ramsbottom in November 2014.

Just beyond the station is 'Victoria Lanterns', the former goods shed now converted into luxury apartments, while nearby is 'The Spinnings', the former Brooksbottom Mill (1876-1987), now similarly reincarnated. Goods traffic from Summerseat ceased on 28 December 1964, though passenger services over the line continued until 3 June 1972. Heading towards Ramsbottom, the railway next crosses the River Irwell on the impressive Brooksbottom Viaduct.

Left: **SUMMERSEAT** is a pretty village popular with visitors because of its attractive scenery and facilities, which include two traditional inns, a garden centre, nature reserve and sculpture trail. A short walk beyond the platform at Summerseat station, the footpath comes into the village near the luxury apartment conversions of 'Victoria Lanterns' (above left) and 'The Spinnings'.

Above: **BROOKSBOTTOM VIADUCT** Making a fine sight as it crosses Brooksbottom Viaduct is BR 8P No 71000 *Duke of Gloucester* at the head of the 11.40 service from Heywood on 23 January 2011.

RAMSBOTTOM The lovingly restored station at Ramsbottom, complete with footbridge, level crossing and signal box.

Continuing northwards the railway climbs steadily to reach the lively market town of Ramsbottom at the heart of the Irwell Valley. The manned station is on Bridge Street and has a ticket office, a small cabin selling refreshments, a waiting room, toilets and free parking for about 30 cars. The popular Nuttall Park is nearby and the Lancashire countryside can be explored from the station by way of the charming riverside walk or the more challenging climb up Holcombe Hill to the Peel Monument.

HOLCOMBE HILL
Towering above Ramsbottom, and with Bury visible in the background, is the impressive monument dedicated to Sir Robert Peel. Standing 128 feet tall atop Holcombe Hill, it was erected in 1852. *Mike Peel*

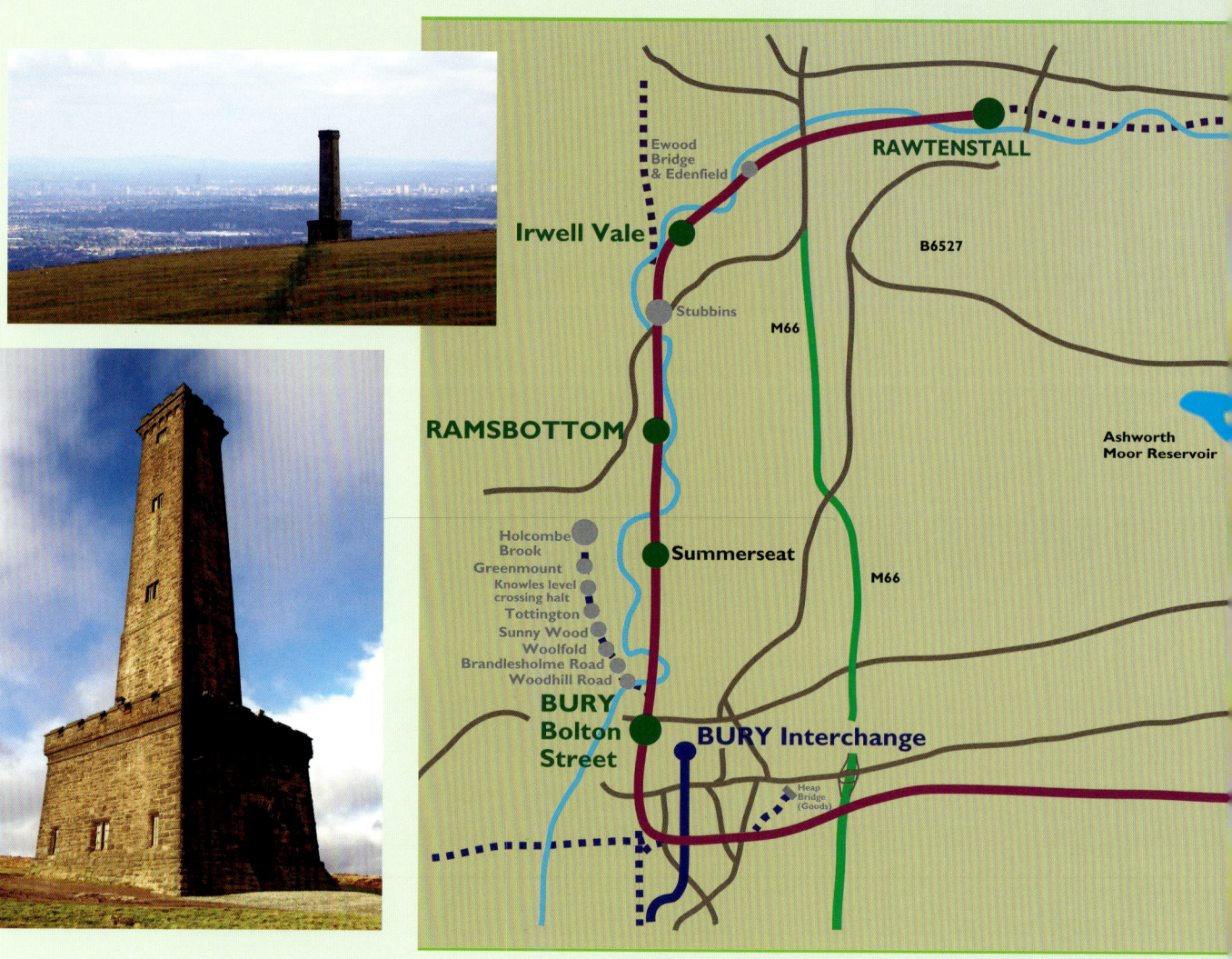

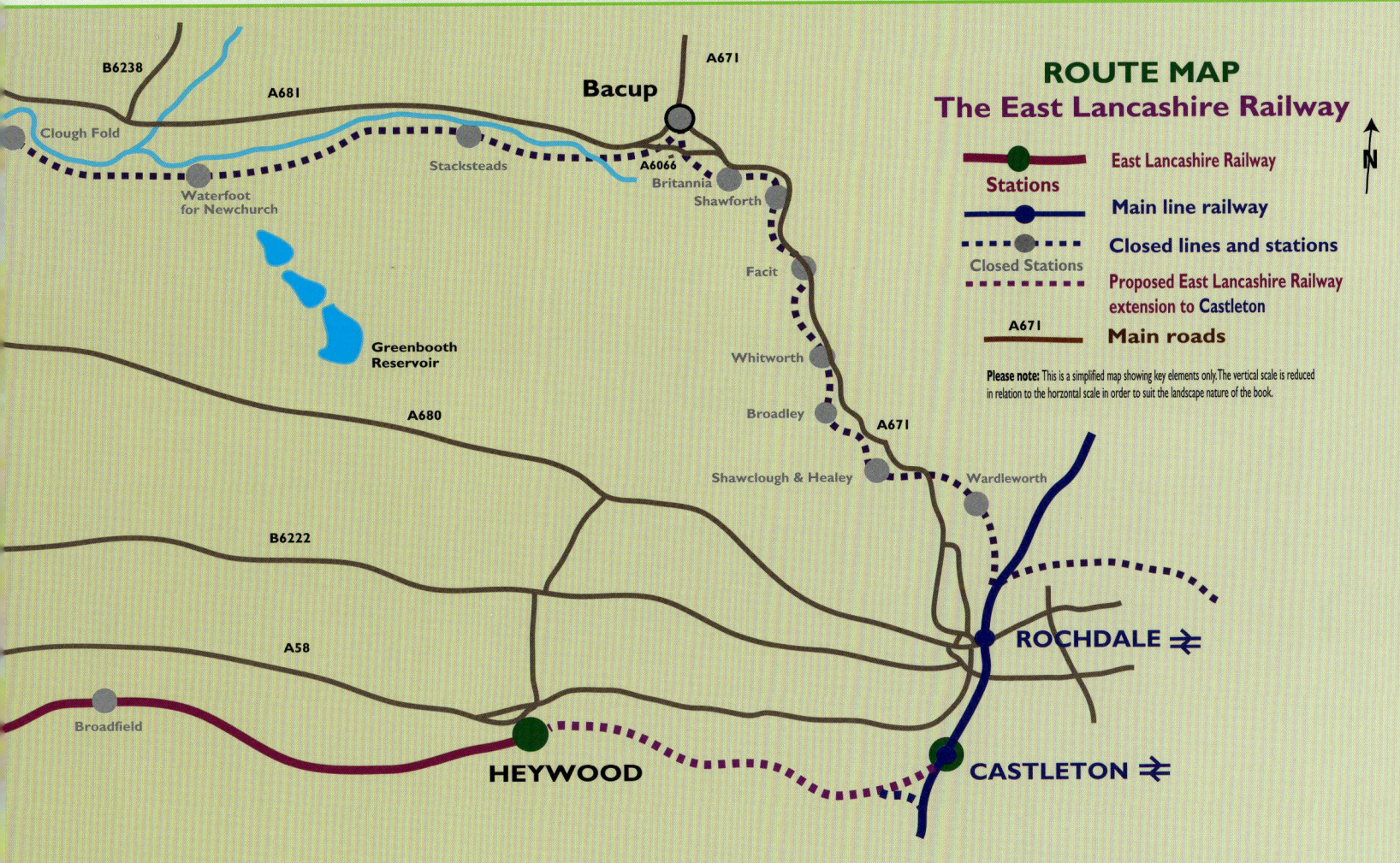

Right: **RAMSBOTTOM** A group of 'locals' wait at the station to board a Heywood to Rawtenstall train headed by LMS 'Crab' No 13065.

Below: **RAMSBOTTOM** Ex-LMS 'Jinty' 3F 0-6-0 No 47324 arrives with a train from Heywood bound for Rawtenstall on 7 July 2007. *Roger W. Haworth*

Below right: **RAMSBOTTOM** It's the little things that make the difference: the platform furnishings at Ramsbottom.

Above: **RAMSBOTTOM**
The small but functional waiting room has a coal fire for those chilly days.

Right: **RAMSBOTTOM**
The single-line token is handed over as 'K4' No 61994 *The Great Marquess* enters the station with a train from Rawtenstall on 1 November 2014.

Above: **RAMSBOTTOM** Trains pass at Ramsbottom on 23 January 2011: BR Standard 5MT No 73129 has brought in a train, the 10.50 from Heywood, and awaits the arrival of LMS 2MT No 46443, which rolls down the hill from Rawtenstall.

Above right: **RAMSBOTTOM** Impatient to be away, the crew of No 73129 wait for the 'all clear'.

Right: **RAMSBOTTOM** Apparently working 'wrong line', LMS 'Black 5' No 44871 is actually on banking duty, assisting No 73129 with her heavy train to Rawtenstall.

RAMSBOTTOM In glorious autumn sunshine, *The Great Marquess* prepares to leave Ramsbottom with a train for Bury and Heywood.

Ramsbottom to Rawtenstall

Between Ramsbottom and the end of the line at Rawtenstall is the second of the unstaffed halts, Irwell Vale, probably the most difficult station to locate by car as it is situated along an inconspicuous narrow road near Edenfield. Irwell Vale is a charming former mill village sitting astride the rivers Irwell and Ogden, featuring well-kept rows of traditional stone-built terraced cottages that recall its former role in the textile industry of East Lancashire. In the nearby Helmshore Mills, now a textile museum, the story of Lancashire's unique contribution to the Industrial Revolution can be explored. Powered by a mighty water wheel, you can see original working machinery that transformed raw wool and cotton into yarn ready for weaving into cloth.

This new station was opened at the same time as the Rawtenstall extension in 1991, replacing one a little further north at Ewood Bridge & Edenfield, which was never rebuilt. There had previously been a goods siding here, complete with a 2-ton crane, but this

Above: **IRWELL VALE HALT** The remote halt at Irwell Vale is to be found at the end of the narrow road through the village. Turn left over the river and continue up to the level crossing.

Left: **IRWELL VALE HALT** LMS 2MT No 46443, on loan from the Severn Valley Railway, is seen near Irwell Vale with the 12.30 service from Heywood on 23 January 2011.

was closed in 1954. This charming little halt has a shelter and a small free car park for about 10 cars. There is a picnic area alongside, but no toilet facilities at this station.

Below: **IRWELL VALE HALT** The ELR's two-car Class 117 DMU, Nos W51339 and W51382, calls briefly at Irwell Vale on its journey back down the valley with the 15.15 service from Rawtenstall on 1 November 2014.

Right: **IRWELL VALE HALT** LMS 'Black 5' No 44871 leaves towards Rawtenstall.

The railway continues its climb through dramatic scenery towards Rawtenstall, the most northerly point on the ELR. A 'typical Lancashire town' with sturdy stone architecture and cobbled streets set among imposing hills, it is the end of the line. Located at the bottom of Bury Road, the manned station has toilets and the aptly named 'Buffer Stops' bar, offering both inside and outside seating. A traditional-style Ticket Office and Waiting Room is situated alongside. On the platform itself, a refurbished carriage, the Rawtenstall Cafe, serves a range of cakes and sweets. Nearby, the converted Lambert's Mill is now an attractive shopping centre, and the Rossendale Ski Centre offers an alternative for the more active visitor.

RAWTENSTALL The approach to the station is controlled by the signal box at Rawtenstall West level crossing.

RAWTENSTALL Southern Railway 'West Country' Class No 34027 *Taw Valley* was temporarily repainted on the ELR and renamed *Hogwarts Express* in 2000 for the promotional tour for *Harry Potter and the Goblet of Fire*. It is seen here approaching Rawtenstall station in the livery that it carried for about a year. *Phil Horton*

Far left and left: **RAWTENSTALL** Stanier 'Black 5' No 45407 arrives at Rawtenstall and runs up to the buffer stops with a train from Bury in August 1998. *Phil Horton*

Below left: **RAWTENSTALL** Crews change at Rawtenstall as No 42765 is prepared for the journey back to Bury. *Phil Horton*

Below: **RAWTENSTALL** The end of the line – Rawtenstall station.

East Lancashire Railway Recollections

Left: **RAWTENSTALL** Passengers enjoy the afternoon sunshine while waiting for their train back to Bury.

Right: **RAWTENSTALL** The well-stocked 'Buffer Stops' bar welcomes passengers and locals alike.

Below left: **RAWTENSTALL** The station waiting room

Below: **RAWTENSTALL** The entrance hall and ticket office.

Below right: **RAWTENSTALL** The clock tower provides both an attractive and useful feature of the main building at the Rawtenstall terminus.

Special events

In addition to the ELR's regular timetable of steam- and diesel-hauled trains that operate throughout the year, a varied and exciting programme of special events offers something extra for everyone, from Gala Weekends featuring 'home-based' and visiting locos (steam and diesel) to family occasions such as 'Day Out with Thomas' and 'Santa Specials'. 'Theme' events also feature, including the very popular '1940s Weekend' and the 'Halloween Ghost Trains', not forgetting the wider transport connection that includes the 'Transport Collectors' Fair', the 'Vintage Transport Gathering' in association with the Bury Transport Museum, the 'Classic Bike Rally', and the 'Lancashire Day' celebration in November. Or why not develop your camera skills with the ELR Photography Courses, held monthly on Saturdays in January, February and March, and on Saturdays and Wednesdays in April, May and June.

BROOKSBOTTOM VIADUCT During a Winter Steam Gala weekend, 'Black 5' Nos 5407 *The Lancashire Fusilier* and 5337 storm out of Summerseat across Brooksbottom Viaduct with their train for Rawtenstall.

The railway has also appeared on film and television, featuring in the 1991 film *Let Him Have It*, the ITV comedy series *The Grimleys* and the BBC1 series *Life on Mars*, as well as in an episode of *Coronation Street*, the BBC film *Eric and Ernie* and a series of episodes of *Hollyoaks*.

Visiting locomotives

The benefits of a connection with the national network have been demonstrated to great effect since the Hopwood link was established in 1993, providing opportunities for the exchange of locomotives and rolling stock between the ELR and other heritage railways.

Top right: **IRWELL VALE HALT** From the Mid Hants Railway, a welcome SR visitor, 'Merchant Navy' Class 4-6-2 No 35005 *Canadian Pacific*, pauses at Irwell Vale.

EWOOD BRIDGE From the Severn Valley Railway came GWR '2800' Class 2-8-0 No 2857, here passing Ewood Bridge.

Below: **RAMSBOTTOM** BR 9F 2-10-0 No 92214, on loan from the Great Central Railway, eases her train out of Ramsbottom.

Diesel Days

It's not all about steam on the ELR. Heritage diesels attract great interest and can be seen at work regularly on timetabled trains and during the popular 'Diesel Gala' weekends.

Right: **RAMSBOTTOM** Leaving Ramsbottom for Rawtenstall across the level crossing, Class 42 'Warship' No D832 *Onslaught* leads Class 52 'Western' D1041 *Western Prince* on 5 July 2007. *Paul Anderson*

Above: **RAMSBOTTOM** No 37109 and the Class 40 Preservation Society's No 345 stand at Ramsbottom on 11 January 2014. *T. G. Ainsworth*

Right: **BRIDGE 18** Type 2 Bo-Bo diesel-electric No D5054 *Phil Southern* crosses Bridge 18 over the Metrolink, with a Heywood to Rawtenstall service on 29 July 2007. *David Ingham*

East Lancashire Railway Recollections

LMS Theme Weekend in conjunction with 'Lancashire Weekend'

Throughout the historic County of Lancashire, many towns host special events on 'Lancashire Day', 27 November, which commemorates the occasion in 1295 when Lancashire sent its first representatives to become members of what became known as the 'Model Parliament', summoned by Edward I with his proclamation 'what touches all should be approved by all'.

Supported by many District Councils, Lancashire County Council and Bolton Metropolitan Council, it was first observed in 1996 with the Loyal Toast to 'The Queen, Duke of Lancaster'. Today the day is widely marked by events that include the reading by Town Criers of the 'Lancashire Day Proclamation', which concludes with the words '…this day shall ever mark the peoples' pleasure in that excellent distinction – true Lancastrians, proud of the Red Rose and loyal to the Sovereign Duke. God Bless Lancashire and God Save the Queen, Duke of Lancaster.'

To celebrate the occasion, the East Lancashire Railway hosted an 'LMS Theme Weekend' on 22 and 23 November 2014,

Above: **RAWTENSTALL** The Class 40 Preservation Society's No 40145 *East Lancashire Railway* stands at Rawtenstall station on 5 September 2007. *JrgNet*

Below: **BURY BOLTON STREET** Class 35 'Hymek' No D7076 departs from Bury Bolton Street on 22 July 2006 with a service for Heywood. *David Martin*

BURY BOLTON STREET After reading the 'Lancashire Day Proclamation' at Bury Bolton Street station on 22 November 2014, Bury's Town Crier leads 'Three Cheers for Her Majesty the Queen, Duke of Lancaster'.

The flag of Lancashire.

BURY BOLTON STREET LMS 'Crab' 2-6-0 No 13065, resplendent in crimson livery, waits at Bury with a service for Rawtenstall.

BURY BOLTON STREET Then the Horwich Prize Medal Morris Men entertain with a display of traditional morris dancing.

which featured three steam locos built for the LMS and representative of types that would have graced the Bury-based railway in the days of steam. LMS 'Crab' 2-6-0 No 13065 (BR No 42765), working in crimson livery, LMS 0-6-0 No 12322, and LYR Class 27, BR No 52322, operated the services between Heywood and Rawtenstall, while LMS 'Jinty' 0-6-0T No 16407 (BR No 47324) operated 'driver for a tenner' duties at Bury station.

BURY BOLTON STREET LMS 'Jinty' No 16407 is about to begin its 'driver for a tenner' programme.

Above: **BURY BOLTON STREET** The crew of the 'Jinty' receive final instructions from Bury's Station Master as they prepare to commence their 'driver experience' duties.

Stock

The East Lancashire Railway owns and attracts a wide range of locomotives, from the recently restored LMS 'Crab' 2-6-0 No 13065 to famous visiting engines such as the LNER 'A4' Nos 60007 *Sir Nigel Gresley* and 60009 *Union of South Africa*. The stock list includes a variety of locomotives including ex-GWR designs, 'Merchant Navy' and 'West County' 'Pacifics' from the former Southern Railway, and an array of LMS and BR types, and although several of these are currently undergoing restoration in the Baron Street shed, any visit to the ELR will be rewarded with the opportunity to travel behind iconic locomotives. The network connection also allows some of the railway's locos to travel elsewhere, either to head main-line tours or to visit other heritage lines up and down the country. In addition to the 'Famous 2' former 'industrial' locos that initiated passenger services on the line in the 1980s, the ELR operates a further two, and boasts a considerable fleet of diesel locomotives and multiple units. A wide variety of beautifully restored coaches and vintage wagons complete the impressive stock list.

The complete stock list is available at www.eastlancsrailway.org.uk/engine-shed.

Right: **BURY BOLTON STREET** As the last of the afternoon sunshine lights Platform 3 at Bury Bolton Street station, the 'Crab' brings in the final train of the day to Rawtenstall.

Opposite: **BURY BOLTON STREET** The 'Crab' prepares to leave Bury towards Heywood, as former LYR Class '27' 0-6-0 No 12322 arrives with a train for Rawtenstall.

Bury Transport Museum

Housed in the beautifully restored 1848 Castlecroft goods warehouse is a fine collection of interactive exhibits and original artefacts that tell the fascinating story of the development of transport in the North West. Situated directly across the road from Bolton Street station, the museum hosts a number of events throughout the year including craft workshops and themed weekends for transport enthusiasts. It is open on Wednesdays to Sundays (and Bank Holiday Mondays) between 10am and 4pm, offering free entry with ELR full line rover tickets. Check for other prices and holiday period opening times at www.burytransportmuseum.org.uk.

Above and right: **BURY TRANSPORT MUSEUM** The Bury Transport Museum is housed in the Castlecroft goods warehouse, and contains a wide variety of exhibits.

BURY BOLTON STREET Waiting outside Bury Bolton Street station to take the last passengers back to their cars parked at Heywood station is a Rawtenstall Corporation single-decker, fleet number 58, of Bury Transport Museum.

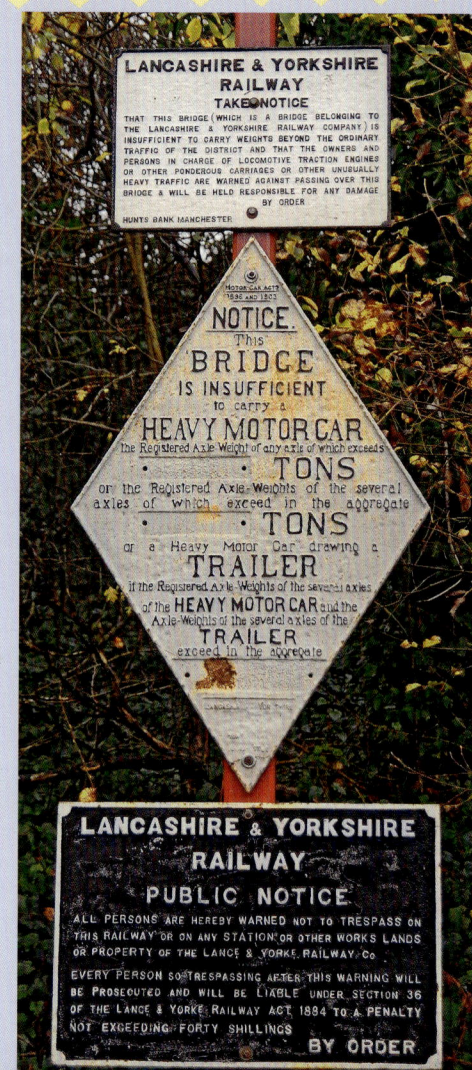

Far left: **BURY TRANSPORT MUSEUM** Also inside the museum are Leyland PS2/1 single-decker MTB 848, Leyland Atlantean PDR 2 No 6809 (TWH 809K); Leyland Atlantean PDR 1/1 No 185 (UWH 185) and Yelloways single-decker NNC 855P.

Left: **BURY TRANSPORT MUSEUM** Among the fine collection of vintage steam-rollers is U 9647, named *Hilda*.

Right: **BURY TRANSPORT MUSEUM** Manchester reversible horse tram No L53 is the oldest vehicle in the museum. It has also been used as a chip shop and part of a hairdressers.

Above: **BURY TRANSPORT MUSEUM** A faithfully recreated warehouse scene.

Left: **BURY TRANSPORT MUSEUM** Dennis F12 fire engine RMB 634.

BURY TRANSPORT MUSEUM Waiting for the train!

Future plans

Included in the '10 Year Development Strategy' announced by the ELR Trust in 2009 are:

- A stop at Burrs Country Park on the outskirts of Bury
- Extension of the railway to Castleton in the Borough of Rochdale, using a new bay platform alongside the main station and allowing exchange of passengers between the ELR and Northern Rail services on the national network
- Further improvement to the station facilities at Rawtenstall
- Replacement of the station buildings at Heywood
- Development of the Buckley Wells Heritage Visitors Centre as part of the target of attracting 200,000 visitors per annum (currently 110,000)

Index

1 (RS&H 0-6-0T) 5
1 (Barclay 0-4-0ST) 9
8 *Sir Robert Peel* (Hunslet 'Austerity' 0-6-0ST) 6
32 *Gothenburg* (Manchester Ship Canal 0-6-0T) 6
2857 (GWR '2800' 2-8-0) 9, 39
3717/3440 *City of Truro* (GWR 4-4-0) 12
3822 (GWR '2800' 2-8-0) 9
4422 (LMS 4F 0-6-0) 10
6998 *Burton Agnes Hall* (GWR 'Hall' 4-6-0) 10
12322 (LYR/LMS '27' 0-6-0) 4, 45
13065/42765 (LMS 'Crab' 2-6-0) 26, 36, 42, 44, 45
16407 (LMS 3F 0-6-0T) 43, 44

34027 *Taw Valley* as *Hogwarts Express* (SR 'West Country' 4-6-2) 35
35005 *Canadian Pacific* (SR 'Merchant Navy' 4-6-2) 39
44806 (LMS 5MT 4-6-0) 7
44871 (LMS 5MT 4-6-0) 29, 33
45407/5407 *The Lancashire Fusilier* (LMS 5MT 4-6-0) title page, 18, 36, 38
46441 (LMS 2MT 2-6-0) 10
46443 (LMS 2MT 2-6-0) 28, 31
47324 (LMS 3F 0-6-0T) 26
53809 (S&DJR 7F 2-8-0) 10
61994 *The Great Marquess* (LNER 'K4' 2-6-0) 21, 27, 30
71000 *Duke of Gloucester* (BR 8P 4-6-2) 22

73129 (BR 5MT 4-6-0) 28
76079 (BR 4MT 2-6-0) 10
92203 (BR 9F 2-10-0) 11
92214 (BR 9F 2-10-0) 13, 40

Class 117 DMU 32
D832 *Onslaught* (BR Class 42) 40
D1041 *Western Prince* (BR Class 52) 6
D5054 (BR Class 24) 41
D7076 (BR Class 35 'Hymek') 41
345/40145 *East Lancashire Railway* (BR Class 40) 40, 41
37109 (BR Class 37) 40